123
SESAME STREET®

PLAY AT HOME WITH ELMO

GAMES AND ACTIVITIES FROM SESAME STREET

Percy Leed

Lerner Publications ◆ Minneapolis

On Sesame Street, there are lots of ways to play and learn! Even when we have to stay inside, the fun doesn't have to end. *Play at Home with Elmo* is a guide for your family to play and learn from the comfort of your home. With your friends from *Sesame Street*, it's easy to make a day at home full of fun and adventure!

Sincerely,
The Editors at Sesame Workshop

TABLE OF CONTENTS

TIME TO PLAY!

You don't need to leave home to have fun. Any day can be a day to play! All you need is a little bit of imagination.

LETTER HUNT

A is for apple core!

Find things in your home that start with the letter *A*. Then look for things starting with the letter *B*. Keep going all the way through the alphabet.

MYSTERY BOX

Have an adult cut a hole in a box. One player puts something into the mystery box. Another player must try to guess the mystery item by feeling inside the box through the hole.

CUP-HANDED ROBOTS

Put a plastic cup over each hand. See what you can pick up with cups for hands! Put each item in a pile. How big can your pile get?

TARGET TOSS

Buckle a few belts into circles. Put them on the floor. Stand back. Try to toss rolled-up sock balls into the circles.

BRAIN BOOST

Make targets that are farther away worth more points. Try to beat your high score!

POSTURE PERFECT

See how far you can walk with a book on your head. Use an open book to start. Then try it with the book closed!

GUESS WHO'S AROUND YOU

One player secretly chooses a person from a group photo. The other players ask for clues to guess which person from the photo the player is thinking of. They can ask yes or no questions only. Can they guess who it is?

Guess who!

GROUCHY PICNIC

One player starts by saying, "I went on a grouchy picnic." Then they add one thing they are bringing, like "I brought my banana peel slippers." The next player adds an item to the list. For example, "I went on a grouchy picnic. I brought my banana peel slippers and broken banjo." Each player adds to the list of items. Try to remember them all.

WHAT'S MISSING?

No peeking!

Set a bunch of items on a table. Have players look at them. Then one player takes something away while the others have their eyes closed. Open your eyes. Try to guess what's missing!

HAT OR NOT?

Find something that's not a hat. Put it on your head! Then take a vote. Silliest "hat" wins!

What a fashion statement!

SPOONAPULT

Make small balls out of paper. Set a few pots on the floor. Step back and sit on the floor. Use a spoon to toss the balls into pots.

BRAIN BOOST
Try to get a ball into the same pot four times in a row.

SINK OR FLOAT

I already know that Rubber Duckie floats!

With an adult, line up items on the edge of the tub. Guess if they will sink or float. Then test them out! Did you guess right?

16

RHYMING SHOWDOWN

Stand back-to-back with another player. Each player takes three steps. Turn around, quick! Each player should say two words that rhyme. The first person to say their words wins.

BRAIN BOOST

If it's a tie, see who can come up with the most rhymes.

LETTERBACK

Using your finger, draw a letter on a player's back. Have them guess what you wrote. Were they right? If not, try again!

SPEAK UP

Say a word quietly. Then say it a little bit louder. See how long it takes for another player to guess the word.

HAT TOWERS

Have one player sit on the ground. Place as many hats as you can on the player's head. See who can balance the tallest hat tower.

Count the hats as you stack! Ah, ah, ah!

KID RULERS

Measure in kids instead of feet! Choose something to measure, like the length of a couch. Have players lie end to end. How many kids long is it?

BRAIN BOOST

What else can you use to measure things?

SUBMARINES

One person is the captain. The others are "submarines." When the captain points up, the submarines rise. When the captain points down, they sink. If a submarine misses an order, they're out!

PLOP! PLOP!

With an adult's help, one player chooses two items that can get wet. Show them to the other players. Then have the players turn around. Have an adult drop the items into the bathtub one at a time. Try to guess which item made which splash.

CIRCLE OF COOKIES

Players sit in a circle. One player starts by saying "nom!" to a player next to them. Players go around the circle saying, "nom!" When someone says "nom, nom!" the direction is reversed. See how long you can go!

BRAIN BOOST

Make a new rule for when a player says "nom, nom, nom!" and play again!

SECRET AGENT MAZE

Grab some tape and string. Have an adult tape "lasers" across a hallway. Duck under or step over the lasers to avoid being "caught!" See how far you can get!

HUMAN LIMBO

Two players make a limbo "pole" by holding hands. Need a longer pole? Hold a mixing spoon between you. Players go under the pole. You can lean back to go under, but not forward. If you touch the pole, you're out! Let everyone go once. Then move the pole down a little. See how low you can go!

BIGGEST BOARD GAME EVER

Make a board game where the players are the pieces! Cut a sheet of paper into four cards. Write 1, 2, 3, and 4 on them. Place T-shirts on the floor to use as spaces. Each player takes a turn drawing a card. Move the number of spaces shown on the card you draw. First to the finish wins.

BRAIN BOOST
Come up with special rules to make the game more challenging!

COOKIE MONSTER CRUMBLE TAG

One player is "it" and tries to tag the others. Once tagged, players must "crumble" like a cookie and lie down. Players can rejoin the game if tagged by another player. The last player to "crumble" is it next time!

SNAIL RACES

Have a race where the slowest person wins! Each player must be moving at all times. No stopping!

THE POWER OF PLAY

USE YOUR IMAGINATION.

Boost your brainpower!
Make sure to play
every day!

GET CREATIVE!

What activities can
you make up to play
at home?

LEARN MORE

Dziengel, Ana. *STEAM Projects 101: Fun Step-by-Step Projects about Science, Technology, Engineering, Art, and Math!* Mission Viejo, CA: Walter Foster Jr., 2019.

Howes, Katey. *Be a Maker.* Minneapolis: Carolrhoda Books, 2019.

Origami for Kids
https://www.origami-fun.com/origami-for-kids.html

Try more fun activities with *Sesame Street*. Have a parent or guardian download the *Sesame Street* Family Play app.

Lerner Publications Company
An imprint of Lerner Publishing Group, Inc.
241 First Avenue North
Minneapolis, MN 55401 USA

For reading levels and more information, look up this title at www.lernerbooks.com.

Main body text set in Mikado a Medium.
Typeface provided by HVD Fonts.

Additional Image credits: fizkes/Shutterstock.com, p. 4; Roman Chazov/Shutterstock.com, p. 10; kritskaya/Shutterstock.com, p. 15; MSSA/Shutterstock.com, p. 20; Picsfive/Shutterstock.com, p. 24. Cover: fizkes/Shutterstock.com; Yuganov Konstantin/Shutterstock.com.

Editor: Andrea Nelson **Designer:** Lindsey Owens
Photo Editor: Brianna Kaiser
Lerner team: Martha Kranes

Library of Congress Cataloging-in-Publication Data

The Cataloging-in-Publication Data for *Play at Home with Elmo: Games and Activities from Sesame Street*® is on file at the Library of Congress.
ISBN 978-1-72842-765-2 (lib. bdg.)
ISBN 978-1-72842-766-9 (pbk.)
ISBN 978-1-72842-767-6 (eb pdf)

Manufactured in the United States of America
1-49331-49446-9/14/2020